Written by Rennie Brown
Illustrated by Stevie Hale-Jones

First published by Parragon in 2009
Parragon
Queen Street House
4 Queen Street
Bath BA1 1HE, UK

Copyright © Parragon Books Ltd 2009

ISBN 978-1-4075-6356-5
Manufactured in China
Please retain this information for future reference

COOL CREATIONS

CREATE THE BAND

PaRragon

Bath New York Singapore Hong Kong Cologne Delhi Melbourne

What's Inside...

ROCK OUT!

Contents

POP STYLE!

How It Works

Check out all the hot style tips in this book, then follow the instructions below to start styling your own chart-topping bands on your CD-ROM!

Using a PC

1. Put the CD into the CD drive.
2. Double-click on "my computer."
3. Double-click on the CD drive icon "Create the Band."
4. Double-click on the "start pc" icon. You will see a loading icon and your CD will start.

Using an Apple Mac

1. Put the CD into the CD drive.
2. Double-click on the CD drive icon "Create the Band."
3. Double-click on the "start mac" icon. You will see a loading icon and your CD will start.

System Requirements

OSX

Apple Mac

- Power Macintosh G4 500 MHz or higher
- Running a minimum Mac OS X 10.2.6, 10.3, 10.4
- CD-ROM drive
- Sound card
- Monitor displaying at least 1024 x 768 pixels in 256 colors

PC

WINDOWS 98 / 2000 / ME / XP / Vista

- Pentium IV processor
- CD-ROM drive
- Sound card
- Monitor displaying at least 1024 x 768 pixels in 256 colors or higher
- 256 MB of RAM (512 MB recommended)

TOP TIP
Once you've installed your CD-ROM, you're all ready to go! If you get stuck, just click the "Help" button on the screen.

Popstar Style

Pop Princess

Microphone headset

Flowing waves

Flowing scarf

Chunky bangles

Short dress

Rock Chick

Wild child hair

Skull motif T-shirt

Long black beads

Cowboy boots

Music is all about style and attitude, and as a stylist you need to think about what look you want! Here's the lowdown on four hot popstar styles.

TOP TIP
Check out these four looks on the CD-ROM first, then try mixing and matching items from the different sections!

Funky Babe

Festival-style sunglasses

Smock dress

Bright belt

Retro denim flares

Soul Sister

Supersleek bob

Gold micro dress

Blinging jewelry

Wide leather belt

Glam high heels

Pop Style Quiz

Can't decide on a look for your band? Don't panic! This cool quiz will reveal a fabulous look to suit your taste!

I think a girl group should have attitude.

Yes →

I like celebs who are totally glam.

Ye

No ↓

Yes →

No ↓

I think Beyoncé is superstylish.

I like guitar bands.

No →

No ↓

No ↓

Yes

I love Avril Lavigne.

Yes →

I like celebs who have their own unique look.

Pop Princesses

No

Bling's my thing.

Yes

Soul Sisters

No

Yes

Yes

Rock Chicks

Most of my clothes are in dark colors.

No

Funky Babes

Pop Princesses

Pop princesses love mixing up different kinds of music on their albums. And they're exactly the same when it comes to fashion. They might wear baxter shorts and tube tops for a dance video, but for slower tracks they might wanna go glam in sophisticated dresses.

Strong lyrics need strong outfits to back them up. Bomber jackets worn with combats or teeny denim minis are a great pop princess look.

Skinny jeans in different colored denims are a great way to bring a band's look together. Team them with cute cropped blazers for a slick finish.

Sassy tube tops look hot with baxter shorts. Go for tube tops in different prints to express each band member's personality.

Rock Chicks

Rock chicks have heaps of attitude and they need a wardrobe to match! Strong designs and deep colors are all part of the image. Rock chicks love wearing slogans, stripy prints, and punky skull designs, so look out for printed T-shirts and dresses.

Try styling your band using a hot pink pinafore dress. Teamed with a pink guitar it'll blow the crowd away.

The punky skull motif on this T-shirt is so rock!

ROCK'S BOLD ROCK'S NOT CUTE

Puffball skirts may not seem very rock chick, but made of black satin and teamed with a purple camisole and a black denim jacket they're totally wild!

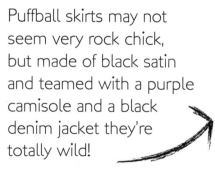

Soul Sisters

Soul sisters love chic sassy designs and glitzy glamor. Look out for micro miniskirts and teeny shorts—these girls wear their denim tight! It's all about making an impact, so pick out show-stopping dresses in metallic fabrics and turn up the heat in colors that zing. Make sure this girl group's outfits are bright and eye catching.

When soul sisters are chilling out in the recording studio, they wear designer joggers and cute little hoodies.

Soul sister chicks look gorgeous in cute babydoll dresses. Team them with sassy cropped jackets and they're ready to groove!

Get your soul sisters looking glam in tropical colored ra-ra skirts and glitzy halterneck tops. Bright colors are perfect for big concerts.

BLING IT ON!

Soul Sister Style

Blinging jewelry

Animal prints

Sleek, sassy hairdo

Denim micro mini

Zingy colors

GET THE LOOK!

TOP TIP
For all the outfits on the CD-ROM, you can pick your own colors and fabrics by using the color bar at the bottom.

Funky Babes

Funky babes play by their own rules. They've got their own sound and their own style. Funky babes love wearing dresses over jeans and totally unique vintage clothes. And a funky babe will only wear outfits that truly express her personality.

Funky babes love cute patterned fabrics! A starry top over a long-sleeved T-shirt looks ultracute.

A belted coat and skinny jeans will keep a funky pop star looking cool and cozy while she's pounding the streets for inspiration.

Opaque tights under a pair of mini shorts are a great look for a fun-lovin' funky babe.

UNIQUE STYLE!

Funky Babe Style

RETRO CHIC!

Funky colored highlights

Vintage cotton dress

Bright beads

Cute polka dot dress

Gladiator sandals

Limited edition boots

Retro denim flares

19

Top Tricks

Popstar stylists have to think about how the look of the group works together. But that doesn't mean dull matching outfits—no way! In their music videos and on stage, each member usually has a unique outfit, but all the outfits coordinate as well. Here are some top insider tricks professional stylists use when styling a girl group.

Dress each band member in the same basic dress, but in different colors, and give each one unique accessories in complementary colors.

Keep it subtle. Dress all your band members in the same basic style, such as this LBD look, but vary the cut and style slightly.

Give each band member a unique outfit, but use the same fabrics across the whole range. A star print will give a look that's totally now.

Tie your band's look together with bold colors repeated across all the outfits. This red and black combo looks awesome!

Think about hair and makeup as well as clothes. All the members of this band have long hair, which gives them real boho chic!

Dress two of your band members using similar colors, and then add a skirt or top in a boldly contrasting color to the third's outfit.

Accessories

Pop Princess Accessories

Plan your pop princess accessories around a particular color theme to give your group a slick finish.

A chunky turquoise bangle, turquoise ballet flats, and a thin turquoise belt all work well together.

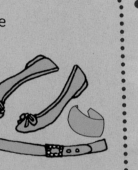

Every pop princess loves the color pink! A floaty pink scarf, a long string of pink beads, and a twist of pink silk can all be used to tie a look together.

When they hit the town for a band night out, even popstars need somewhere to keep their makeup! Pick out a pretty clutch and a purse bag.

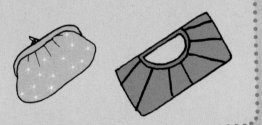

Chunky plastic bangles in funky colors are a great accessory for your pop princess band. Pick out a few colored bangles for each of the girls to wear.

Rock Chick Accessories

Get the rock chick look by picking out strong accessories to team with your outfits. Look for buttons with slogans printed on them. They look cool on your coat, your bag, or your guitar strap!

Cowboy boots are classic rock footwear. Search out a beaten-up vintage pair. Lace-up boots are another style essential. Why not use purple ribbons instead of laces?

Buttons are a rock chick essential! Pick out designs that suit the personalities of your band members.

Plastic bangles are totally rock if you choose the right colors! Pile on loads of black ones and pick a few in shocking pink or purple.

Accessories

Soul Sister Accessories

The soul sister's key accessories are diamante and gold. If it sparkles—she'll wear it!

Can you get gold cowboy boots? A dedicated stylist will look everywhere for the right accessory! Strappy sandals are another must-have for this chick. She's just crazy about shoes!

Diamante necklaces give the girls the sparkle they love. Look for hearts on long chains and letters on silver chokers.

Soul sisters love bags almost as much as they love shoes! Pick out a different-colored clutch bag until you find the best choice for each girl's outfit.

Funky Babe Accessories

Funky babes love interesting and unusual accessories. A funky babe is just as likely to wear her granny's old brooch, as she is expensive designer jewelry.

Funky babes often play at cool outdoor music festivals. A pair of gladiator sandals is perfect for these gigs!

A funky singer needs somewhere to keep her notebook when she's writing lyrics for her next album. Go for a cute bag in an unusual or vintage fabric.

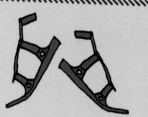

Beaded bracelets and bangles look great when they are all mixed up together. Wrist cuffs and sweatbands are another funky choice.

Band Beauty

Of course, every girl group needs to look fab on stage. But beauty products are also a secret weapon for any good stylist. A makeup look can say as much about your band as any outfit.

Pop Princess Beauty Tips

Pop Pout
Pop princesses love to shimmer and shine. Keep your lips slick with tubes of gorgeously fruity lip gloss.

Expressive eyes
Pop princesses love experimenting with colored eye shadow. Electric blue, emerald green, bubblegum pink are all big faves.

Rock Chick Beauty Tips

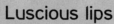

Luscious lips
Put aside your girly shades of pink and coral! Rock chicks like dark lipstick. Black cherry, deep scarlet, and purple lipstick are top rock colors.

Chart-topping cheeks
Rock chicks wear a lot of black and they can easily end up looking a bit washed out. Apply a hint of blush to warm up their complexions.

Soul Sister Beauty Tips

Polished nails
Soul sisters take their nails seriously. They love going to the nail salon to have the latest designs painted professionally.

BLINGIN' NAILS

Sassy eyes
The soul sister eye shadow palette is full of sassy browns, dark blues, and charcoal grays.

Funky Babe Beauty Tips

No limits lips
There are no rules with a funky babe. When she wears lipstick, she goes for a bold bright shade. And while eye makeup looks cool on her, she doesn't wear it at the same time as lipstick. She's just not into wearing a lot of makeup all together.

PUCKER UP!

Funky nails
When it comes to nail polish, this girl is totally out there! She loves painting her nails surprising and unusual colors.

Hot Hairstyles

Pop Princess Key Hairstyles

Sky-high ponytail
A high ponytail is perfect for a pop princess group's energetic dance routines.

Lovely layers
Pretty layered hair is a great casual look for a pop princess group. It's great with either straight or wavy hair.

Rock Chick Key Hairstyles

Wild child hair
A long layered look with unusual color highlights is sure to attract attention. Keeping hair slightly messy rather than slick and groomed is all part of the look!

Funky quiff
This quiff is a fab retro look that recalls the days of old-time rock 'n' roll. Your band will look like they should be playing with Elvis with this hairstyle!

Soul Sister Key Hairstyle

Side-swept bangs
Sleek and glam but with a unique twist, side-swept bangs are a supersassy look for a soul sister.

Textured bob
Uneven bangs and loads of choppy layers are a great way to wear chin-length hair. This is a more relaxed look for chilling out in the studio.

Funky Babe Key Hairstyles

Boho braids
Cute and kooky braids are easy to do and create a cool hippie vibe for your band.

Pixie crop
A short wispy crop is a great look for funky independent babes.

Video Shoot

You've created an image for your pop group and styled them to perfection—it's time to set the cameras rolling and pick a venue to shoot their chart-smashing hit. Which shoot location suits their image?

LOCATION:
Times Square
Glam, exciting, and just a little bit edgy, shooting your video in the middle of a big city can be a great choice.

LOCATION:
Moonlit Forest
A forest is a dramatic location for a music video shoot. The cameras love a beautiful moonlit night. Add a couple of silver-gray horses and you've got the ingredients for a magical pop video!

LOCATION: Tropical Beach

If your pop group's recording a tune to top the charts over the summer, then pick a relaxed beach location for their shoot. Just make sure the outfits are right—a glam evening dress on a beach might look a bit funny!

LOCATION: The Red Carpet

Only VIP pop stars can walk up the red carpet to this exclusive star-studded event. Make sure your pop stars do signature poses and talk to the crowds while the photographer gets his shots.

LOCATION: Japanese Garden

This dreamy Japanese-style garden is a perfect location for a pretty, romantic video shoot. Coordinate your band's outfits with the flowers in the garden for a fabulous effect!

TOP TIP

Want to make some funky invitations? Create the funkiest girl group you can then print them out and use them as invitations!

Print Band

When you're finished, you can print out your group.

TOP TIP

For every band you create you have the option to fill out a fact file about them including the band name, members' names, music style and stylist's notes.